Bittersweet Beauty

by Lacie Shea

Prologue

Bittersweet Beauty is my third poetry book, but unlike *The Weighted Heart* and *Burn Marks*, I didn't break this book into sections. When I write, I never set out with a particular theme in mind. Instead, I sit quietly, watch the shadows crawl across the wall and imagine what my heart would say. It's sometimes heartbreaking, other times introspective, occasionally political, cheeky, but always honest. The poems collected here are my daily confessions; small vulnerable moments that found a soft place to land and a chance to breathe on the page. And while there are definitely reoccurring themes, there's a beauty in leaving it up to the reader to decide where the poems should fall. And if I've learned anything on this journey, it's that poetry speaks its own language and it's not always the writer who translates it best.

To my mom, for always picking up.

And to Jess, that joint book tour would have been the best.

I fear this heartache is so deeply burned into my chest that the wound will never heal and I'll forever wear smoke for perfume and tears as pearls.

-Heartburn

You kissed me

You were scared

You missed

It was clumsy

And awkward

With a weird side hug

But you kissed me

I was scared

I turned

It was perfect

And sweet

With a warm side hug

But you kissed me

You kissed me

- Practice makes perfect

Let's kiss under the moon and make the stars jealous.

-Until the sun comes up

May you live so well that bad decisions,
become your favorite stories to tell.

-It's all part of the fun

Full confession – I dream about you

But don't tell anyone. I don't want to stop.

-Can't wait to go to bed

How selfish of me to want you,

but there's just something about having my cake

and eating it too.

-It's my party and I'll cry if I want to

Whisper it to me in poetry

-I'm listening

Let's make the world wait, while we write poetry and talk about love.

-Take a number

I have a real distaste to Mondays. They steal the covers and you.

-Mondays suck

I'll make you a deal. You return my heart and I'll give back the butterflies.

-Yes, I know it's broken

There is so much more to us

More we can't say

More we can't do

More we can't be

More *I want you*

-I want seconds

We were meant to go down in flames,

but I'm sorry I set fire to the bridge.

-Shouldn't play with matches

Let's pretend it's Sunday and let the sheets kiss our skin,
while we kiss each other.

-Almost hump day

How terrifying to have my head in agreement with my heart.

-What she said

Whether this ends in a moment or forever, I will carry you always.

-Once in a lifetime

How perfectly you love my imperfection.

-Human

How difficult it is to see through the butterflies,
with these rose colored glasses.

-See what I want to

It might happen. I might bump into you on the sidewalk, coming round the corner in a big city, far from anywhere that makes sense. You'll be alone, in between somewhere you had to go and somewhere you have to be. I'll be on my way to grab coffee; one more moment alone, before needing to get back. Our eyes will meet, you'll say hello first and I'll immediately blush and look down. There will be awkward small talk, a few oddly placed compliments, questions about one another's family. You'll tell me you were hoping to grab coffee too and I'll invite you to join me. You'll offer to buy mine, but I won't let you and we'll wait for our names to be called. "It really is good to see you." You'll say. "Thank you." I'll reply. And in the quiet, between that sentence and the next, we'll say all the things we wanted, buy never did. "It's good to see you too."

- Chance meeting

She doesn't love quiet, but she won't apologize for being loud.
The world is better for hearing her heart.

-Turn it up

How delicious it is to wear fantasy; to put it on and pretend.

To imagine the people we could be and the places we could go.

-Dress-up

You've officially become a "Happy Birthday" text.

-Make a wish

I like the unexpected things that remind me of you;
that my heart finds you in places I wouldn't think to look.

-Green hearts

How beautiful she is to have tears as unapologetic as the rain.

-It's raining. It's pouring

Oh, but I haven't forgotten. That's the trouble.

-If only it was that easy

Goodbyes aren't forever.

I've never lost someone and not found them again

in music, poetry or rain.

-Lost and found

Why would I divide my wish for you amongst the stars. Let me shout it to the moon, with her magic to control the tides and light to guide lovers home.

- Miracle worker

We can be over. We can be done. We can end.

But please…

Don't ever be finished with me.

-Bottomless brunch

Maybe I said too much. I do that you know,

leave my heart cracked open;

moments folded over

and people bookmarked.

-Open book

I no longer feel welcome here. Strange to be a stranger in my home. I drag my fingers along the hallway and let them disrupt every newly hung painting. Only two channels on the TV now; one static, the other black and white. The food in the fridge isn't to my taste and the milk has spoiled. Upstairs the photos of my family and friends have been removed. No warm smiles to greet me. In my bedroom, the bed is smaller and the curtains don't open to the light. My bedside table is missing my books and it's not my clothes in the closet. No familiar smells or laughter rising from the kitchen. No comforting arms to fall into. Strange to be a stranger in my house. I'd offer to move, but I think they've already moved on.

-New locks

I don't want a fairytale. I want the hard and the dirty. Let's set fire to our souls, so we may rise from the ashes. We will dive headfirst when the world dares us to jump from castle walls and will slay dragons with our tears. Let's leave our crowns on display and break every royal decree. We will fight to our deaths. But, you will be mine and I will be yours and we will be real.

-Happily ever after. The end.

Maybe I set my pen down, give the ink time to dry.
My hand is stained, the pages smudged and
the sun is out.

-Where are my sunglasses?

Meet me here love, where lies don't cling to truth. Where doubt doesn't linger in the space between your words. Meet me where certainty easily settles and trust isn't ashamed to be seen. Meet me when answers flow as steady as questions and worry can't catch-up. Meet me here love. Sit with me. Hold my hand and tell me it's ok to stop holding my breath.

-I want to believe you

I wish you could hear the way I remember you.

Maybe then you'd miss me too.

-Selective memory

I've done my best to stitch this broken heart back together, but there are days when my missing you is so strong that it rips through the seams and again I'm in pieces.

-Patchwork

I miss you

I love you

I want to call you, but…

I can't

I won't

-I'll just internet stalk you

How lonely it feels next to you.

-See through

Shit! This halo is heavy; tempted to say fuck it and ask the devil for a ride back to your place.

-Hey. Can I ask a favor?

Today I pack this chapter, these moments, these choices, this version of myself; I no longer have the space for what was, I need room to grow.

-Movers are here

The devil on my shoulder has a lot to say about you.

-All good things

Careful.

Your fantasies are showing.

-Blushing

So what is the meaning of life?

"That's easy," she said. "It's you sitting here with me,

 having conversations like this."

-Sunday afternoon

The what isn't.

The can't be.

The never was.

The if only.

The hasn't happened.

The won't be.

The might have been.

-I miss you…

It's quite possible that I may drown in these tears, but still,
I sit and cry rivers in the rain.

-Higher Ground

She will always be here. I watch her you know, see how she flirts with you, teases you. What's one kiss? Two? What is it about her that blinds you? That convinces you that somehow you're allowed us both? Each time you bring her to your lips...
How lonely it is to love you. How hard it is to watch you curl around her, while you're lying next to me.

-Mistress in a bottle

Do you want to tell them they can stop playing our song
or should I?

-Dancing with myself

Have you heard the rumors about us?

I kinda love them.

-Let's keep them talking

Let's go for coffee; my lips can speak of insignificant things, while my eyes plead for attention and my hands dream of holding more than a cup.

-It's never just coffee

How soft and lovely the daydreams of you

Like wild flowers and cashmere

Linen and lace

Sun kissed shoulders, on summer nights,

 beneath Christmas lights

-How very lovely

It wasn't you who woke me, but the birds who wouldn't let me sleep. The dove calling for her lover. The impatient sun pulling at the covers and the song of morning traffic. And though, the air was cool and begged me to stay with my daydreams, my eyes had decided. But then they saw the coffee you'd set on the nightstand and felt the warm smile on my lips, and agreed to a few more moments. So I took my time, prayed for the dove and hoped the sun would understand.

-Morning can wait

But then we dance in the kitchen to some forgotten love song, from when everything was perfect and butterflies existed and forever felt easy.

-Is something burning?

I signed *xoxo* and you signed your name.

- Just kidding

I woke up to a note from you. I woke up to what was, to what I imagined. I woke up and got coffee in the kitchen and stood at the sink I waved to someone who's name I should remember, but can't. I thought about breakfast. Poured more coffee; feels cold for May. I opened and closed the fridge. I looked at the fruit bowl, the bananas are going brown. I thought about getting ready; I think the clock is slow. I woke up to a note from you. I woke up to the old me.

-"Alexa play my October playlist."

This is when you choose to tell me you love me. When the house is on fire and the zombies are at the door. There's a tornado forming in the yard. The wheels have fallen off the car. Aliens are landing. The monster under the bed is real. I've lost my ability to scream. Only corn in the cupboard. I started a new job. I hate my hair. They're canceling my favorite show. I finally stopped needing you. And this – This is when you tell me you love me?

-Your timing is impeccable

I wish I'd written more about the love and less about the missing.
To remember what it was and to forget how much it hurt.

-Love poems

It's not the weight of the world on my shoulders, but the weight of these obsessive manipulative thoughts that settle heavily upon me. An ache that crawls from my mind and permeates deep into my chest, pinning my lungs and binding my heart. It's a seemingly continuous exhaustive battle to shake them. To convince them that there isn't a reality to cling to; a reality to make a home in. How I wish to simply brush them off, ignore their relentless negativity.

Stop…

Stop…

Stop!

It's never loud enough to drown them. They only rest, before gaining the strength to start again.

-Wanna be Scarecrow

What a magical spell those stars cast, making us believe we were written for them.

-View from the top

You feel like the summer I turned 16…
Windows down, a favorite song on,
tan lines and coconut.

-Meet me at the beach

She struggled with goodbyes, because of how easily she loved.

-I promise to write

What is this pen on paper, but an echo of a memory. Whispered mentions of moments, made of magic, melancholy and madness.

-Dear diary

Find me between the light and dark,

Within the dusk and dawn

Where everything is about to begin and there's no sadness in the end.

-The gray

Maybe my French will improve. Maybe I'll learn to love tea.
Maybe I'll find a favorite pub. Say soccer when I mean football.
Spend hours lost in museums. Fall in love with a bookstore. Visit
the home of my great grandfather. Write a novel along the Thames.
Have snow at Christmas. Vacation in Iceland. Ireland. Lose myself
on cobblestones. Miss the sun. Run into you.

-When in London

For a moment I had you. In the city lights, in the loud music, in the spilled drinks, in the summer heat, in a memory.

-The dance floor

To all the mistakes I've made wanting to be loved, may you find a place to call your own. A home far from guilt and full of forgiveness.

-Sit by the fire

It's ashes from memories burned that color my ink.

-Burn marks

I thought I'd rush to cover these walls, but there's something about sitting here in a sunlit room with nothing to see, but the newness of it all.

-Hi. My name is

There's something deceiving about moving to a new city and not knowing a soul, as if you can be a stranger even to yourself.

-Haven't met her

How loud the rain is; like change.

As if I need more of a reminder than the puddles at my feet.

-My socks are wet

She preferred sad love songs. Even when happy, she saw the beauty in the pain.

-Love a good cry

I don't think I'll ever repaint that picket fence.

- Who cares what the neighbors think

And then she put down the phone and picked up a book and found how easy it was to turn the page.

-The push of a button

You know that favorite dream? The one you can't explain. The one you beg to have when the night feels long. The one that feels like you got lucky, like magic exists. The one you roll over in your mind wanting just a few more memories from. The one no one will ever understand. It's like that. You remind me of that.

-Last night

I think there's something beautiful in the idea that we learn the most about ourselves in imperfections; in the hard and dirty; in the scars we earn. That most of what shapes us is unplanned. That heartbreak teaches us more than butterflies and that grief doesn't exist without love. I like knowing that mistakes mean change and that losses grow determination. Missteps improve balance. Regret asks forgiveness. Fractures can heal and broken can mend.

-Made whole

How unexpectedly sharp; the corners of my memories.

-Ouch

Questions and 2 a.m. thoughts are what remain of my memories of you.

-Still in my head

How much easier I thought it'd be counting years instead of days, but that's the thing, I'm still counting. I still count the distance between you and me.

-365, 366, 367, 368

I chose to tell you I was ok, because I knew you'd choose to believe it.

-I'm fine

I've broken up with jealousy too many times to count and still I go back; those green eyes, the fire she ignites, the self-doubt she brings; she pulls me in every time.

-God damn she's good

I want them back; my words. Their confessions, their stories, their pain, their truths – My heart. I need them back. Give it back.

-I said too much

I stripped off every vulnerability, while you threw dollars at my feet.

-Free drinks

It was just as you said it'd be, but without you.

-Couldn't help but think

How different these chapters; how thin the pages between them.

-Filler

This tangible divide. The day and night. Right and left. These exhaustive extremes, so loud as to drown out both the up and the down. Red and blue make a dark purple bruise. This fracture, both sides painful to the touch need time and truth. We cannot heal, if we refuse to look at the wound.

-Jan. 7th

And then there are those nights when your memory is so seductive that I curl into possibility and play with *what if.*

-Satin sheets

I just need to have one too many drinks and a conversation that lasts past 2 a.m.

-Who's counting?

And I'll wear black, because that's how you remember me

-How do I look?

I think love looks most beautiful dressed in the everyday.

-You wear it well

The dream was so real that I thought we shared the memory.

-Get into my car

How silly to search for you in love poems, when you're so easily found in those that speak of heartbreak.

-Peekaboo

Sometimes I miss my broken heart

and all the beautiful things it had to say.

-Healed

I think one of the greatest fears in love is being forgotten. The idea that what was, wasn't. That maybe it didn't mean what you thought. That maybe they didn't love you the same. That when they think about love, they don't think about you.

-I was there, I should know

How loud the night

How quiet the moments

-DJ! Turn it up!!!

Not all love stories are written into forever. Some of the greatest love stories ever told are found on pages of moments; a look, a smile, a touch. Unfinished chapters, with favorite memories folded and *almost* bookmarked.

-Can't put it down

I shall clean my closet of skeletons and make space to forgive myself.

-No longer haunted

I like that we'll always have one day.

That one day we met.

The one day we might meet again.

-Street corner

I love how you read my poetry with whiskey in your eyes and coffee in your cup.

-Careful, it's hot

My days are outlined with memories of you. How careful I am to stay inside the lines.

-Sharpie

Please don't call. You'll wake the butterflies.

-Let them dream

A lifetime ago. Yesterday really. Three months from now. Last night. Two weeks from Tuesday. The day before yesterday. Tomorrow. This morning. In four months. Before dinner. A year, no two. This coming Thursday. A second ago. In five minutes. Today.

I missed you.

-Always

She's the kind of girl that daydreams of sun kissed skin, while catching snowflakes on her tongue.

-You should still wear sunscreen in the winter

How loud the night with whispers of the unsaid.

-I saw that going differently

So…in the next lifetime, what do you think? Your place or mine?

-I have Netflix

How deliciously syrupy sweet the thoughts of her. Sticking to every second, of every moment, of every day.

-Pancakes at noon

Christmas is coming, you'll be busy

I'll run into your mom and she'll ask how I am

And you'll be busy

I'll go to that party and have too much to drink

And you'll be busy

I'll take a selfie and think I look pretty

And you'll be busy

I'll crawl into bed and play that song

And you'll be busy

I'll text you I miss you

And you'll be busy

-Did you get my Christmas card?

I hope to one day give you a smile that says, I remember everything.

-Say cheese

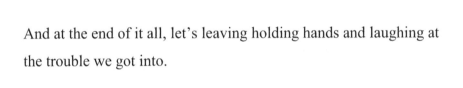

And at the end of it all, let's leaving holding hands and laughing at the trouble we got into.

-I'll get your coat

My favorite song came on and you turned it up.

-I don't know the lyrics

I've named all of my scars.

I earned them.

They're mine.

-Let me introduce you

What's your poison…

You.

It will always be *you.*

-I need a chaser

We were more than friends.

Not quite lovers.

We didn't have benefits;

Just butterflies.

-And BBQs

Tied up to you with double knots of memories and maybes.

-Right over left

I want to make it hard for you to hold back a smile when they ask you about me.

-Why are you smiling?

You slipped though my fingers like ribbons of silk.

Too beautiful to catch.

But oh…

To have touched you.

-Too fast

Time always calls your name.

-Let's take attendance

How perfectly you fit between the girl I thought I was and the woman I've become.

-Detour

Unanswered love letters and a heart littered with paper cuts.

-What remains

I like the maybe, the wistful thinking, the playful daydream; something to slip into at dawn and wear with my first cup of coffee.

-The best part of waking up

Hey it's me. I know it's been forever and that we're more strangers than lovers now, but maybe we could go for coffee, maybe find a moment somehow.

We could meet at that place on the corner, the one just down from you. Remember we'd go there, when things were shiny and new.

I think it'd be nice to reminisce, smile at the past, reflect on bittersweet moments, ignore why it didn't last.

They say there's something healing about looking back, at appreciating how far you've come. Actually...

Umm...

You know what.

Forget the coffee. It's not fair for me to interrupt.

I guess; I guess it's a good thing you didn't pick-up.

-After the beep

Those 2 a.m. conversations with you. As though my soul is no longer lost in translation.

-A.P. Literature

I'd like to think that you think of me. And I don't mean obsessively or longingly, but that on occasion, on any given day, a bit of nostalgia hits and for a moment I'm there; for a moment a piece of gum, a chocolate shake, a missing button becomes magic.

-A cocktail napkin

Can you imagine if we had kissed??

It's good right?

Like, we would have nailed that shit.

-Champions

There's a streetlight just outside my window. I guess it's there for comfort, to keep the dark away, but there are some nights, when it sneaks through and wakes the loudest of thoughts. It stretches across my bed and pokes at every self-doubt, every opened wound, every bit of missing until it forces sleep to leave me and I'm left with tangled sheets and tired eyes.

-Power outage

And now that I've wrung your memory dry; it's time to let go and make new ones.

-When life hands you lemons

I thought my birthday maybe. Christmas or Valentine's; your birthday. The first day of summer. When that band came to town. The election. After that one actor died. Taco Tuesday. Covid.

I don't know, I guess, I just thought, you'd find a reason.

-Text me

She wrote love letters on paper airplanes and hoped for answers in bottles along the sea.

-High tide

Let's pretend. I'll be waiting for a train and you'll be headed home; I'll bump into you and you'll look at me and we'll fall madly in love all over again.

-Come here often?

Sometimes I wonder how permanent these memories are, like the tattoo on my arm; deep beneath my skin, a reminder of my former self, easy to hide, but not to forget.

-Laser removal

And for a moment we were both lost

At the same time

At the same place

Before you turned left and I turned right

-MapQuest

And I think I'll only ever speak to you again in poetry; find you in poetry, but what a beautiful way to say goodbye.

-Folded corners

Winter is calling. I can hear the leaves dragging their feet; how curious that they too should resist change.

-To every season

Always at the foot of my 2 a.m. thoughts; whispering soft memories; keeping the ghosts away.

-Tuck me in

Sometimes the halo doesn't match the outfit.

-Try the horns

I love wearing nail polish with suggestive names. Give me a lackluster pink, with a name like, Angels Corruption and I'm all in.

-Can you hand me my keys?

How heartbreaking that the best news should become the worst
without you to tell it to.

-You would have picked up

I'll set this love here. Take it as you need; as telegram or time capsule; in this lifetime or the next.

-Open when necessary

And then it was over. From a moment to a memory.

-Remember when

How easily love letters climb from the box beneath my bed
hoping to find you.

-Maybe I should close the lid

I even miss your goodbyes.

-Good night sweetheart

And what of those memories that you never put down. Those worn and warped, polished with overuse. Overplayed, but never played out. Those memories that flush your cheeks and lick your lips and tell your heart to run from what is and race to what was and remind you of life lived. Moments that hang breathless, Magic minutes made immortal. Sensual seconds that tease time and beg for a redo.

-Sorry, I was distracted

It's officially been years. What a difference a seemingly simple, sad, silly s can make.

-The letter of the day

It was nothing, but something.

-Nothing really

How terribly self-destructive she's become, trying to turn moths into butterflies.

-Dust

I can't remember our last phone call. I hate that I didn't store it away for safe keeping. That though I run my mind over every mundane moment, I'm unable to touch the topic of conversation. There must have been a hello in there, and I'm sure it ended in good-bye, but my greatest hope is that *I love you*, found its way in.

-Ok, I love you

It's my own fault, this permanence of you, from where I held on a little too long, a little too tight.

-That's going to leave a mark

I used to look at old pictures of myself and only see hurt looking back. Shame. Regret. A smile that could hide all of it. But now, when I catch those eyes, from a seeming lifetime ago, I see determination. Strength. A force to be reckoned with. She may not have known where to go or how to move forward, but she did. She kept going. She carried me and she fought to get me here. No, I no longer see her pain, I see her, the warrior.

-I love her

There are pieces of me that miss the girl who told easy lies and smiled to hide the truth.

-I felt prettier

I keep cigarettes in my drawer; I'll never smoke them, but I like to think that somewhere I'm wearing red lipstick, cheap perfume, black lace, tempting fate.

-I have tattoos you can't see

You used double knots when you tied me with that string of wild.

-Can't shake it

On days when my scars ache to be touched, I'll play songs that trace my memories and pull at my seams if only to feel you again.

-Sometimes I don't want to be happy

Tell me about the poems you've left on the page, the poems that haven't found their way to someone else.

-Lined paper

I don't drink whiskey, but there's a piece of me that's drawn to who I imagine I'd be if I did. Someone who devours Dickens, next to a crackling fire, in a worn leather chair. Or who wears a ballgown, with cowboy boots, every Tuesday, on the Upper East Side. Or who when the air smells like rain, they find themselves on the hood of their car, talking to the stars with Patsy Cline whispering from the radio. I don't drink whiskey, but I do own cowboy boots.

-On the rocks

You really shouldn't have. They're lovely.
But I just don't have space for butterflies.

-My favorite gift, but my god they're messy

Made in the USA
Las Vegas, NV
19 December 2023

83139331R00089